MY CHAOTIC POINT OF VIEW

A POETIC PERSPECTIVE

C.C. SUMMERVILLE

Dedicated to Keira & Kylie.

A personal notation from the Author:

Poetry has been my outlet from my early teens into my thirties. This is a collection of my writings throughout the years. I hope that my insight and point of view might inspire others to write and depict their own point of view for the world to see.

I can't tell…

I can see them coming,
racing down the hall,
laughing and giggling.
Oh no, they're coming to talk to me.
"I heard something that Judy told me,
that Susan told her,
but I can't tell."
Now they prance off.
"I can't tell." "I can't tell."
Those words buzz around by head.
I curiously trot to class.
I think to myself as the teacher rambles.
"I can't tell." "I can't tell."
Why can't I concentrate?
Those words won't leave.
What could it be?
What did she mean?
"I can't tell." "I can't tell."
The day slowly rolls on.
Class after class,
teacher after teacher,
blah, blah, blah…
"I can't tell." "I can't tell."
Some say words can't hurt,
others disagree.
I'm one of the others.
Words are like knives…
Be careful how you use them.

Life

The beginning is seen through your mother's eyes.
The end is always unknown.
We are told to live today like it's your last,
but I'm not going to die tomorrow!
Crashes, overdoses, kidnappings,
rapes and murder.
None of those things could happen
to me!
I'm full of faith, love and trust.
I surround myself with kind
and loving people.
BUT life is unpredictable
and what goes up must
come down.
The people closest to you
could die tomorrow.
Then what?
Pretend you can't feel the pain?
Go numb?
Cry away the memories?
Or maybe just run?
Never take one moment granted!
Everyone dies, but...
Not everyone truly lives.

The Cycle

See the good.
Hear the bad.
Tell the innocent

They say…

They say the times are just
so tough…
They say my life could not
be rough…
They say I'm too young
and cannot know.
They say I must find
a way to grow.
Time is not on my side,
is experience?
I've seen things
that others have not.
I've learned things
that most will not.
But…
They say I'm too young
and age never lies.
I say, STOP…
Take a deep breath
and open your eyes!
Those who watch and listen,
gather and grow
become wise beyond their years.

Neglect

Shhh...
Don't talk,
don't move,
don't dare!
Pretend you're invisible.
Pretend they're not there.
Pretend you don't care.
Why would you bother?
Why would they notice?
Why are you there?
Neglect!

Within

The innocent by standard.
The viciously accused.
The angry convict.
The crime.
The lies and deceit.
How do we know them?
They all lye within.
Who are you letting out
today?

Define me...

Am I my possessions?
My looks?
My jokes?
My friends?
Would I be described by
my hopes
or dreams
my achievements
or failures?
Remember my regrets?
When was it fun?
Did you think I was cool?
Who spread the rumors?
Did that put my name
in the books?
The present turned past.
People and places.
Events and mistakes.
Old friends forgotten.
Strangers now held close.
Say the truth,
don't dare lie.
Pretend it won't hurt.
Define me...

Siblings and Love

I thank the heavens above
for these amazing people
who would lie, cry and die for me.
All out of love.
Growing up,
I can't believe we made it out
ALIVE.
Friends, fights,
drama, dares,
stress, strains,
emotions and enemies.
How did we manage
to survive?
Making it through everything
TOGETHER
with my siblings and love.

My Advice

Passing judgement
won't change your life.
Acting better
won't make you better.
The lie will never
become reality.
Embrace who you are.
Find the good in others.
Our lives will never
show complete perfection.
Dream big!
Laugh hard!
Help when you can.
Except change.
And when you find love,
cherish it!

Change

Feel the need for a new
energy, a new force.
The deep longing for change
and the despair from the
same old, same old.
Turn the page,
Where's the next chapter?

~Mind Warp~

Fantasy, reality,
ecstasy.
I can't see
what you see.
Insanity!
Colors and shapes,
places and lines,
anger with rage,
tears and sighs.
Comments run long,
advice ran by.
Who am I today?
Where am I tomorrow?
~Mind Warp ~
Faces with names.
This place...
hard to explain.
Grasp the wheel,
pretend to know.
Time passes by,
numbers get larger
and some move on.
The end has come.
What's next to face?
~Mind Warp ~

Addiction

The craving,
that need.
His body...
That food...
The drug...
My regret,
that feeling,
the pain.
Mine.
Yours.
Theirs.
We all have them.
What's yours?
How well do you
control it?
Self-destruction.

Love

Sometimes one sided.
Always intense.
Life changing,
mind altering,
emotional ties.
Love.
Falling,
feeling
and seeing.
Friends,
families
and lovers.
Feelings evolve.
People change.
Life never stops.
Love it to the fullest.

Wonder

This person, I seem to know.
I stare blankly and wonder
how the mind works.
Could it be changed?
Who's in control?
When is enough?
Where will I let go?

You

Too afraid to let anyone in.
You broke through my walls.
As I pushed all others away,
you managed to show
genuine friendship and care.
Turning lust to love,
passion to affection,
and my life to ours.
The changes that I never expected
came wrapped up in you!

Had

I had a spark
and it fizzled.
I had a dream
and it faded.
I had a muse
and it vanished.
I had a wave
and it crashed.
I had a light
and it went out.
We had an us
and you damned it.

My View on Death

Knowing that death is approaching is a gift not all will receive.
The darkness could be creeping and lurking around any corner or shadow.
Bound to hit at any unexpected second or moment.
Some go in pain, suffering until the very end.
Others find luck and go on in a drift or quick shift all at once.
You're gone, but still there remains the pail and sick version of what once was.
Sadness and pain rain all around.
Could it be worse to die or to see all that remain morn?
Follow the light and see where you headed.
To dance upon clouds or dream about heaven.
Forced to view all your wrong doings.
I could preach on religion,
tell right from wrong,
and say I know Jesus and God.
Would that help?
Saying I know everything's fine is ignorance bliss.
Death could be the passing of one life to the next
or a sentence of eternity.
What you believe may be true,
but how long will it carry you?
Will you hold it in your heart when the one nearest and dearest is forced to pass and wait for you?
Could the vale drop and show you another side?
Making you the next visionary and leader?
Follow your heart,
but soon you will be met with your own great
END.

Me?

Can I trust you?
Do you know?
Could I show you?
Do you see it?
I want you to be the one.
To believe.
To confide.
To recognize the real me.
I keep her inside.
I'm scared of the truth.
Of the person I could really be.
Is that me?
Am I the monster?
Are my thoughts real?
I feel the hate,
the anger,
the rage.
Where is the light?
What do they see,
say
and think?
Who am I?
Me?

Alone

Stand in room full of
faces with names
and yet be alone.

Feel the emptiness
in a well strung out
conversation.

Receive a compliment
and feel it pound you
to the ground.

Stare in the mirror
and not know or understand
the stranger with an empty gaze
before you.

When was the slip
that sent me spiraling
down this black hole?

Could I ever find the light?
Is it really out there?
If I do, will I know?
So many questions unanswered
and much more I will never
come to know.

My confusion ran long.
With no good advice.
But feel this emotion
and know that you are not alone.

Me or You

Can you contemplate
this concept?
Let it swirl around
your mind.
I'm here now
and you set me
to the side.
I left yesterday
and you thought
you had died.
You explained
to me
the pain of suicide.
So I ran back
in a hurry.
And here I am,
lost in my thoughts
of what could have been.
What I let slip
through my grasp.
Like the sand
that runs
through that
damn hour glass.
Have I wasted away
to my worries of you?
What have I put myself
back into?
Who do I choose?
Me or you?

Cycle-Broken

To every end,
new beginning.
To every death,
new life.
The cycle
keeps going.
Could we fall through the cracks?
Slip under the second hand?
Never to be seen
or heard from again?
After winter
comes spring.
The calm
after the storm.
Could the tornado winds
sweep us away?
Get stuck in the chaos?
Feel the burning need
for it day to day.
Has your chaos
become
your reality?
Unstick the glue.
Reach out for help.
Every day is an
opportunity for
change.
Life a new!

Fate?

Sit back and try to relax,
but feel so much pressure
that you might just collapse.
The weight on your shoulders
has built up as boulders.
The stress just keeps eating
but the heart stays strong beating.
Why am I here?
Just pass me beer!
I want to forget
and do anything that I'm sure to regret.
As the buzz washes over
I seem to recover
but the night flies right by.
And with the morning
comes the why.
I hear all the stories
and try to swim through
my blurry memories.
But all that returns are the reasons.
Ready for the next drink.
I sit back and think
"Where is my break?"
What path must I take?
Have I worn out my chances?
As I daze in their glances,
others believe my fake pleasant mask
that has fulfilled its only task.
So I'll sit back and try to contemplate
my way out of this terrible fate.
If all else fails, I'm sure to drown
with all that ails.

I'm Out

Your words said one thing
but your actions told another.
This sequence of events
has created a complex.
I replay the events in my mind.
Could I ever hit rewind?
Re-record, remix, re-do?
I wanted the truth.
Straight up!
Will you ever
take off that mask?
Let me see
the real you?
If it's all just a front
I'm out, call it quits.

Thoughts

My mind
races
and yet...
All of my
thoughts
lead back
to you.

Forget It!

Twisting and turning.
The light keeps on burning.
And in chime the voices
that keep on urging,
encouraging, disturbing the
peace I thought had existed.
Damn! I guess I missed it.
The events feel so distant.
I should have resisted.
Now caught in this web.
Or is it all in my head?
Have I over read?
Misconstrued, misunderstood
that facts that I thought were hard as wood?
Forget it, it's all good!
Keep up the straight face.
Try to stay ahead in this
rat race.

Blur

Thoughts
wonder...
Eyes glazed.
Concentration
set aside...
Where has time gone?

Enough

As I wash my hands
of this mess,
the blood sweat
and tears
run off with the fears
and worries of what
I have caused.

The realization
has settled.
The facts all came out
and left me without
any doubt.

To you,
I abandoned
but I had to escape
before you could
lock me in with your fate.

I'm free
but still look back.
I will miss you
but know you
would never change.
I could not force it
or save you.

-Wishing love was enough.

Misunderstood

Out and around,
sideways and upside down,
space and air,
the middle
and in between,
across the intersection,
down that crazy lane.
Here you stand...
Lost, beaten and
misunderstood.

Lost Memory

I left that place.
Have the thoughts
of me followed?
Do you push me away
into the black space?
Or am I that knot,
too difficult to be swallowed?
Could I be that
"what if"
that keeps you awake?
The last vague thought
before drifting off to sleep.
Or have I become
just another lost memory.

I Want to Explain

I want to explain.
I want you to know.
I feel it inside.
The conflict that won't subside.
Should I cope
or call it quits?
Give in to the voices?
Leave all the worries and chills.
I feel the eyes upon me.
And wish I could
hear the voices inside.
I wonder with great despair.
I know I will never be told.
I feel the sharp pain
and just think to myself.
If the rage were to
bubble and blister
could it explode?
What would it cause?
Massive chaos
or just another angry
look of discussed?
Could it be the cause of my slip
and spiral to this dark place?
I want to explain!

Played

I was accused
as you twisted
my mind.
I sit back and
wonder...
what did I decide?
I was really played!
This is how feels.
My anger
was overcast.
How could
this happen?
How did you
get in?
Re-lock the door!
I won't
look back!
Call me a hermit,
a shut in,
but this shit
will NEVER happen
again!

Reality

Are we all really here?
The confusion mixed with wonder.
Do we all really exist?
Could this many people really coincide?
Each face has a story.
One I will most likely never know
and they will never know mine.
Is this all a dream?
Has my consciousness created these faces?
The thoughts are perplexing
and the possibilities seem never ending.
One conspiracy theory after another.
How long until a conspiracy becomes our reality?

New Beginning

Feeling the shift of a new chapter.
The cool breeze or refreshing wave.
Knowing that the past is over
and you've begun life anew.
The excited anxiety
of new challenges and adventure.
Reminding yourself that you'll have to behave.
The emotions,
so hard to contain.

My Babies Eyes

I stare into my beautiful baby's eyes and I am in awe of
their potential.
I am enamored at the great possibilities and wonder
that awaits.

Where is the balance?

As parents we are busy, rushed, exhausted and pushed
to our limits.
Our homes, cars and minds are a cluttered mess.
We push ourselves to the limit to do the best we can for
our children;
who need us to keep going.
The struggle is real...
As we watch our beautiful children grow and become
more independent,
we have more time to keep up with life
and yet start to miss our babies, the mess, the chaos...
Where is the balance?
Does it exist?
The struggle is real...

I’m Working On It...

I would like to think this is all means to an end...
That all of my hard work will soon pay off...
That I am making all of the right choices
and one day I will look back and know I did it...
I succeeded and bettered myself,
not only for me but for my family and children...
One step at a time...
I'm working on it...
I'll get there...
I just need to figure out where...

www.ingramcontent.com/pod-product-compliance
Lightning Source LLC
LaVergne TN
LVHW020543160826
845677LV00015B/4170

* 9 7 9 8 4 1 0 0 2 2 7 0 5 *